HOW TO BEHAVE IN A CAVE

It's What You Do In The Cave
That Gets You Out Of It

by
Cathy Duplantis

Harrison House
Tulsa, Oklahoma

Unless otherwise indicated, all Scripture quotations are taken from the *King James Version* of the Bible.

Direct quotations from the Bible appear in bold type.

How To Behave in a Cave—
It's What You Do in the Cave That Gets You Out of It
ISBN 1-57794-311-2
Copyright © 2000 by Cathy Duplantis
P.O. Box 20149
New Orleans, Louisiana 70141

Published by Harrison House, Inc.
P.O. Box 35035
Tulsa, Oklahoma 74153

CONTENTS

&. &. &.

CONTENTS

CHAPTER 1

SO YOU'RE IN A CAVE! NOW WHAT?

J esus said that in this world we would have tribulation. But He also said, **Be of good cheer; I have overcome the world** (John 16:33).

Sometimes bad things happen in life, and you just want to retreat. (Have you been there?) In this life, the devil sends all kinds of tribulation your way to try to make you run and hide in a cave.

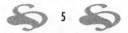

Perhaps fear, discouragement, failures or disappointments are driving you into a cave. Or maybe battle fatigue is making you faint along the way because you're so weary in well doing. (Gal. 6:9; 2 Thess. 3:13.)

But the Bible is full of reasons for good cheer. You don't have to stay in a cave. You can come out, once and for all, and be victorious. God wants you to get up, stand on your feet and go forward with Him.

IT CAME TO PASS AWAY

When your back is up against the wall, you don't have to give up; you don't have to pass out. No matter what it is that has come against you, it didn't come to stay. It came to pass away.

Sickness didn't come to stay in your life. It came to pass away, in the name of Jesus. Failure didn't come to stay. It came to pass away, in the name of Jesus. Any problem you can think of didn't come to stay. It came to pass away, because Jesus declared,

Heaven and earth shall pass away, but my words shall not pass away (Matt. 24:35).

So whatever it is that comes against you, you can say, "That thing is in the earth, and it's going to pass away. I'll have victory over it, because the Word of God is going to dominate this area of my life. And His Word will *never* pass away!"

A LIFE LESSON

I don't know about you, but I like life lessons. Years ago I heard a story that is still one of my favorites. It's one I've often told my daughter to teach her that she can overcome any problem and that she doesn't have to get down when troubles come.

A little bluebird was flying around in a pasture one day. It was snowing and the little bird got so cold that he couldn't fly anymore. So he landed on the field and began to freeze.

The snow kept falling until, eventually, he was completely covered with snow. Just about

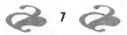

the time he thought he was going to die, a cow wandered by. It stood right over him and dropped a great big plop on top of him.

At first the little bird was aggravated and mad because it stunk. He said, "What is this?" But after a while, he thought, *Hey, this isn't too bad. It's kinda warm.*

The frost started falling off of him, and before long he began to revive. When he realized that he was going to live after all, that little bird was so happy he began to sing and chirp up a little song.

The little bluebird was just chirping away when, all of a sudden, a fox nearby heard him. The fox ran toward him, dug him up and ate him.

And so the moral of the story is this: Not everybody that dumps on you is bad. Not everybody that picks you up is good. And if everything is going great, then for goodness' sake, keep your big mouth shut!

Everyone in a Cave Isn't Bad

That's not exactly a scriptural lesson for your life, but it does illustrate something I saw in the Bible about three men in a cave. They also learned a great lesson in life. They learned that not everybody who winds up in a cave is bad!

You see, it's the *devil* that's bad. But God is good, and He will pick you up when you are down. That's the kind of God we serve.

I'm telling you, when things look their worst, God is always ready to pick you up. He will illustrate in His Word what you need to do to come out victorious.

Even if you're at a point where it seems you've fallen and you're trapped in a cave of discouragement, you don't have to stay there. If you keep your eyes focused on Him and don't give up, you're going to win every single time.

Stop beating yourself up and thinking how bad you must be, or how terrible your life is, and start packing your bags and getting ready to go. God always has a way, and He wants to bring you out of whatever cave you happen to be in.

So if you're in one right now, wondering what you're going to do, then read on. You're about to learn how to behave in a cave and how to come out in victory!

CHAPTER 2

❦ ❦ ❦

DAVID:
FIVE KEYS TO VICTORY

Remember those three men in a cave I mentioned at the end of chapter 1? Well, they weren't actually in there all together. I was talking about three different men in caves on three different occasions: David, Jonathan and Elijah. But the important thing is, they didn't stay there. *They came out!*

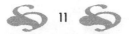

All of them learned principles on how to get out of their caves. And you can apply the same principles that they learned to your own situation.

So let's start with the first "caveman," David. As you read on, you'll notice I've devoted several chapters to David's life. That's because, written in the Psalms, we have his personal record of survival through the caves of life. So we can learn a lot about how to behave in a cave from this one man whom God loved.

DAVID'S ESCAPE TO A CAVE

Most likely you've heard the story of David, the little shepherd-turned national hero. When he knocked down the giant Goliath with a stone and a slingshot, he became the talk of the town. People started singing about it in the street—how Saul had killed his thousands and David his *ten* thousands. (1 Sam. 18:7.)

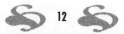

12

Well, do you know what? They should have kept their big mouths shut! They sang so much, it infuriated Saul. He became consumed with jealousy and wanted to kill that little guy. So David was running for his life.

According to 1 Samuel 22:1, **David escaped to the cave Adullam....**

But he didn't go there alone.

When his brethren and all his father's house heard it, they went down thither to him. And every one that was in distress, and every one that was in debt, and every one that was discontented, gathered themselves unto him; and he became a captain over them: and there were with him about four hundred men.

1 Samuel 22:1,2

Four hundred men went with him. However, they weren't exactly the kind of people you like to surround yourself with when you're going through

13

a trial. Usually, when you're down, you want to try to find people who are up.

But here David was, surrounded by people who were in distress, in debt and discontented. These guys were losing at the game of life.

FROM FAILURE TO SUCCESS

But God specializes in transforming failures into successes and turning losers into winners. Something happened to those men when they followed David into that cave. They may have been discouraged when they went in, but I tell you what, they didn't stay discouraged. They didn't stay in debt, distress and discontentment. God showed them how to get out!

In fact, they became so strong and courageous that the whole world came to know them as "David's mighty men." (1 Chron. 11:10.) They were so success-ful and blessed that they joyfully contributed out of their vast wealth to finance the building of the temple of God. Now that's success!

But just as David and those 400 men discovered, there are some key things you have to do to go from being a loser to a winner and from failure to success. They had to learn how to behave in a cave.

You see, there were certain principles that they applied during those early days that established a firm foundation for their success. And we're going to find out what they were.

OUT OF THE CAVE, INTO VICTORY

A careful examination of Psalm 57 reveals five important keys to successful behavior in a cave. This psalm is David's record of his own thoughts when he fled from Saul into the cave of Adullam.

Be merciful unto me, O God, be merciful unto me: for my soul trusteth in thee: yea, in the shadow of thy wings will I make my refuge, until these calamities be over-

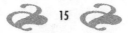

past. I will cry unto God most high; unto God that performeth all things for me. He shall send from heaven, and save me from the reproach of him that would swallow me up. Selah. God shall send forth his mercy and his truth.

My soul is among lions: and I lie even among them that are set on fire, even the sons of men, whose teeth are spears and arrows, and their tongue a sharp sword.

Be thou exalted, O God, above the heavens; let thy glory be above all the earth.

They have prepared a net for my steps; my soul is bowed down: they have digged a pit before me, into the midst whereof they are fallen themselves. Selah.

My heart is fixed, O God, my heart is fixed: I will sing and give praise. Awake up, my glory; awake, psaltery and harp: I

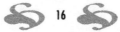

myself will awake early. I will praise thee, O Lord, among the people: I will sing unto thee among the nations. For thy mercy is great unto the heavens, and thy truth unto the clouds. Be thou exalted, O God, above the heavens: let thy glory be above all the earth.

Psalm 57:1-11

In this powerful psalm we discover five things that David learned:

1) He learned to take refuge in God.

2) He learned to cry out to God.

3) He learned to declare God's promises.

4) He learned to expect victory.

5) He learned to give praise to his God.

These keys led not only David but everyone around him out of the cave of Adullam and into victory. In the following chapters, we're going to study each one of these five keys so that we, too, can

behave appropriately in a cave and then follow our God's lead into victory.

CHAPTER 3

CRY OUT TO GOD, YOUR REFUGE

Be merciful unto me, O God, be merciful unto me: for my soul trusteth in thee: yea, in the shadow of thy wings will I make my refuge, until these calamities be overpast.

Psalm 57:1

David made God his refuge. He learned to put his total concentration on God and to trust Him, which paved the way for his success. It was the first step to his coming out of the trouble that he was in.

Once David made God his refuge, calamity had to go. He said, "I'm going to make God my refuge *until these calamities be overpast.*" In other words, he recognized that his calamity did not come to stay. It came to pass away.

HIDDEN IN GOD

You know, when calamity comes, some people feel like all is lost and they're all alone. But when you make God your refuge, you'll never be alone.

David may have thought all was lost, but because he made God his refuge, he was not alone. You may think, *Of course he wasn't alone—not with 400 men hanging around!* But even surrounded by people, a person can still feel alone. But David was not plagued with such a feeling of loneliness.

You see, in the physical, David was hiding in a cave. But in his heart he was hiding under the shadow of God's wings. That's where he was abiding. So, as far as David was concerned, he was *in* God.

In the natural you may be in a hospital bed or at some low point in your life. Or you may be in the cave of sickness or discouragement. But it doesn't matter what your situation looks like. If you are making God your refuge, then when you look at it through the eyes of your spirit, you're not in a cave: You're in God.

The Word says, **If any man be in Christ, he is a new creature** (2 Cor. 5:17).

It's when you're in God and in Christ and when you realize that all those things are temporary that God begins to pave the way to your success. And when you make Him your refuge, He will always bring you out victoriously. Give glory to God because every calamity *has* to go away when you take the first

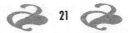

21

step of abiding under the shadow of His wings *until these calamities be overpast.*

CRY OUT TO GOD

The second step to your victory is crying out to God in your moment of discouragement. First, you make God your refuge until everything else dissolves away in the spirit realm. Then, when your eyes are focused only on God, you cry out to Him.

David learned early in life to cry out to God. He made prayer his commitment in life. It wasn't just something he did when he was down or in trouble. It was his lifestyle.

He did it when he came against the bear and the lion; he did it when he came against Goliath. (1 Sam. 17:34-51.) And when he came against King Saul, who had made him his enemy, David cried out to God again. He said,

I will cry unto God most high; unto God that performeth all things for me.

Psalm 57:2

A TENDER HEART FOR THE LORD

I don't think it's a hard thing for us to turn to God in times of trouble and cry out to Him. Most of us know how to cry out to God. And by *cry,* I don't just mean raising your voice; I mean actually letting out some of those tender emotions—such as love, gratitude and trust—and maybe even some tears before the Father.

For some reason, women seem to have an easier time at this. At least, I know crying has never been a hard thing for me. Just get me started talking about how good God is and what He's done in my life, and it's all over.

When I was first born again, I went to a little church that had testimony services, and I always wanted to testify. They'd ask, "Does anybody here have a good testimony?" and I'd always raise my hand because I had so much to be thankful for.

In those services, different people would stand up and testify. There were those who could just

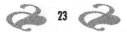

praise God and go on for ten minutes, exhorting and praising God, and the whole congregation would get excited.

Then there was this other type of person who would get up and be so boring that everybody would fall asleep.

And then there was me. I'd get up and say, "I want to thank the Lord," and I'd just start crying. I wanted to give God praise and glory for what He had done in my life. But every time I stood up, I couldn't even talk.

I'd just be able to say, "I want to thank the Lord...." Then I'd burst out into tears as the whole congregation stared at me.

People would come up to me after the service and say how much my testimony blessed them. I'd look at them in disbelief.

"Are you kidding?" I'd say. "I couldn't even get out a sentence."

"Oh, yes, but your heart just blessed me so much."

I used to talk about it to my mother-in-law. I was just so frustrated. I told her, "I don't know why I can't say a word in church."

She said, "Cathy, that's the golden finger of God touching your heart."

I said, "Well, I wish He'd touch my *tongue* so I can say something!"

I remember the day I finally said more than "I want to thank the Lord." I actually got an entire sentence out without breaking down in tears. I was so pleased that God was answering my prayer.

People came up to me afterwards, sort of congratulating me on being able to get out that one sentence. I don't know if they were blessed so much because of what I said or because I'd actually broken through that six-word barrier.

But, you know, as much as I used to hate it, I've come to appreciate that tenderness before the Lord.

I'm just so grateful that His hand still touches me that way, even though I don't always know when it's going to happen.

Usually, when I talk about our testimonies—how my husband, Jesse, or I was born again—I'll cry like a baby all over again. So sometimes I'll try to avoid sharing those things when I'm speaking so that I can at least get out a complete sentence.

So I learned to flow in the Holy Spirit. After all, that's really what counts—whatever *He* wants to do. And He does it, glory to God!

I told the Lord, "Have handkerchief, will travel." In other words, anytime He's ready, I'm ready.

I think that is so important. We need to learn how to stand strong and cry out to God.

It takes a big man to cry. But the Word says Jesus wept before Jerusalem.

I tell you, when your heart is open and transparent before God like that, He just pours Himself in. Sometimes your flesh can't handle His almost tangible presence and you'll just break out into tears, crying and weeping before the Lord.

THE CRY OF INTERCESSION

It's an awesome thing that happens when we make ourselves vulnerable before the Lord in prayer. I read the autobiography of Charles Finney, a great American evangelist who knew how to cry out to God in prayer. He said there were times when he would just weep before God on his face, interceding and pouring out his whole heart before Him with groanings that couldn't be uttered. (Rom. 8:26.)

As a result, he had some of the most spectacular moves of the Holy Spirit. Whole cities were born again through his ministry. He told awesome stories of the hand of God moving when he'd pour out his heart. He'd cry out to God because he had a heart for souls. He cared about the people who didn't know Jesus.[1]

27

That's the way we need to be. We need to cry out to God, whether we're the ones in the cave of discouragement or we see others in that condition. Too often when we see people going through troubles, we just point out the gap, instead of standing in the gap and crying out to God for them.

WHEN YOU POUR OUT, GOD POURS IN

We need to pour ourselves out into others' lives by crying out to God for them in prayer. I heard a story about John Wesley that said he had a terrible wife and that she tormented him beyond measure.[2] But the interesting thing was that, despite any terrible thing she may have done, he attributed most of his success to her.

Some people think that they can't be effective because of their circumstances. For instance, they may say, "I can't do anything for God because my wife (or

my husband) isn't supporting me. She (or he) is not behind my ministry."

John Wesley never said anything like that. In fact, he said, "She kept me on my knees—and because I was on my knees, I had victory every day of my life."[3]

This is the same man who would go out into a field and thousands of people would come to hear him preach. People would ask him, "How do you get such huge crowds?" And he'd say, "I set myself on fire, and people just come to watch me burn."[4]

He got that fire while he was on his knees praying in the Holy Spirit and crying out to God. God poured a fire into his bones that could not be shut up. (Jer. 20:9.) And because of the power of prayer, people came and their lives were changed.

THE POWER OF FERVENT PRAYER

You should never underestimate the power of prayer. It parted the Red Sea. It raised the dead. It has always brought victory everywhere it has gone.

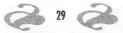

That's what prayer has done and will continue to do—even for you!

When you cry out to God, He makes a difference. When you fervently cry out to Him, nothing is impossible.

James 5:16 says, **The effectual fervent prayer of a righteous man availeth much.** And then to illustrate how effective the fervent prayer of a righteous man is, the Bible gives the example of Elijah, one of our three "cavemen," whom we will study more closely in chapter 7.

Elias [Elijah] **was a man subject to like passions as we are, and he prayed earnestly that it might not rain: and it rained not on the earth by the space of three years and six months. And he prayed again, and the heaven gave rain, and the earth brought forth her fruit.**

James 5:17,18

Elijah was a normal man who, just like you and I, had passions and shortcomings. He wasn't always perfect. But the Bible says that when he cried out to heaven, it did not rain for a space of three-and-a-half years. And when he cried out again, the heavens poured out rain.

The very heavens can respond to a person who cries out fervently with red-hot petitions to God!

That's what David learned when he was in that cave. He cried out to his God—the One whom he knew would perform all things for him—and God answered!

There is power in prayer that is available to every one of us. It wasn't something that was just for a special few, like the prophet Elijah or King David or John Wesley or Charles Finney. God wants us all to stand strong and have a life committed to fervent prayer and crying out to our refuge—because that's the kind of prayer He responds to.

CHAPTER 4

§ § §

DECLARE THE
PROMISES OF GOD

I will cry unto God most high; unto God that performeth all things for me. He shall send from heaven, and save me from the reproach of him that would swallow me up. Selah. God shall send forth his mercy and his truth.

Psalm 57:2,3

When David began to declare that God would perform all of His promises for him, he was still in the cave. So it didn't *look like* any of those promises were being performed. But he began to declare it even before he saw it.

That's the next key to your victory: Begin to declare God's promises *before* you see them.

David declared, "My God performs *all* things for me!"

God is an *all* God!

The Bible says that Jesus healed *all* who came to Him and that He healed *all* manner of sickness and disease. (Matt. 12:15; 4:23.)

It also says **all things are possible to him that believeth** (Mark 9:23) and **God shall supply *all* your need according to his riches in glory by Christ Jesus** (Phil. 4:19).

I'm telling you, God is an *all* God! And there is nothing that is impossible to the person who learns

to take refuge in Him, to cry out to Him and to declare His promises.

FROM SMALL BEGINNINGS...

Declaring His promises means filling your mouth with the Word of God. I learned years ago that my words were containers that hold my future, so if I wanted God's promises to dominate my life, His Word would have to dominate me. I had to learn to let God's Word become the final authority in my life and I had to begin to declare what I wanted.

I'm famous for making lists, and I used to make up long lists of things that I was expecting God to do for me. Then I'd verify them by finding Scriptures of what God had promised concerning each request.

It didn't matter whether it was healing, provision, favor, guidance or just wisdom on how to do a certain thing. I'd seek out treasures in God's Word about it and keep a record of the hidden things that God

revealed to my spirit as I spent time crying out to Him.

I would put those precious promises on my refrigerator door, where I could always see them, and I'd begin to declare them.

That's what I did when we were outgrowing our first home and believing God for our second. Jesse and I owned a tiny little 900-square-foot, two-bedroom house. Jesse was a nightclub entertainer and we traveled all over the country, virtually living in hotel rooms, so we thought that little home was an adorable little cottage. We were glad to have it. But after a while it got kind of cramped.

When we first started Jesse Duplantis Ministries, I ran a day care in that little home, and during nap time the borrowed typewriter, which was hidden underneath the bed, would come out. I'd write letters to pastors or do whatever I needed to do for the ministry during those times.

The end tables in our living room were actually record albums. Twenty years ago they were the big thing.

Jesse did a lot of singing in the early part of his ministry, and we believed God for the money to record his first album. But then when the albums came out, we didn't have anywhere to put them. So I stacked them two across, two back and about five high, put a little cloth over them, and they became my end tables.

I would praise God whenever they sold. Of course, our tables kept getting shorter and shorter, but I was glad to see them go.

So, you see, we really had a small beginning, but the Bible says we're not supposed to despise small beginnings. (Zech. 4:10.) God honored our steps, and He did some awesome things back there in that little house.

But we had gotten to the point where we needed another home because our beloved cottage was so

crowded and Jesse needed someplace where he could study the Word when he came home from revival meetings.

In those days Jesse held revivals, which usually ran Sunday through Wednesday. When he came home he'd tell me stories about what had happened and I'd get so excited.

I wanted to be able to go with him, but I couldn't.

We just had one little car, which Jesse drove to the meetings. All of his albums would be piled in the backseat, his little sound system was in the front, and the trunk was loaded with everything else. I couldn't have gone with him because there was no room!

We didn't know a lot about prosperity in those early days. But we've learned a lot since then, and God has brought us a long way. (That little car sure was a blessing though, because it took only a cup of gas to fill it up!)

PUTTING GOD FIRST

When Jesse was on the road, my daughter Jodi and I were always faithful to go to church and put God first. I had friends who would drive us once in a while, but they weren't always as committed as we were and sometimes they'd miss church.

I was determined never to miss church. I hated to miss. I never wanted to miss out on what God was doing. So I arranged for the church bus to pick up Jodi and me. We'd ride that bus to the service, get fed and be blessed.

I'm telling you, we were dedicated. Still are. We did whatever needed to be done to serve the church. We were just like Isaiah. You know, "Here I am, Lord. Send me." (Isa. 6:8.) Sometimes we didn't even know what we were getting ourselves into. But we stayed committed and involved in the church, doing whatever our hands found to do. And God was always our first priority.

We found that whenever you make yourself available to God, He gives you abilities you didn't know you had. He's just looking for people who are available, and that's what we were.

That's how our ministry began. We had a small beginning, but I'm telling you, God rewards faithfulness.

KEEP HIS PROMISES BEFORE YOU

As I mentioned, I learned to declare God's promises even way back then. I drew up a little floor plan for the house that we were believing God for, and I noted all the things I wanted—every single thing: I had three bedrooms, a study and even a garage (because I wanted to be able to stay out of the weather when I got in and out of the car). I mean, I put everything down.

Then I wrote out all of my Scriptures and put them right beside my floor plan. I still remember one of God's scriptural promises that I wrote down:

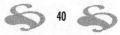

40

Through wisdom is an house builded; and by understanding it is established: And by knowledge shall the chambers be filled with all precious and pleasant riches (Prov. 24:3,4).

Then, after I finished drawing up the floor plan and writing down the Scriptures I'd found, I wrote "Subject to change by the Master Builder"—not because I didn't think God would meet every need, but because I didn't want to limit Him.

Whatever God wanted to do was all right with me. I figured He might want to make something up or add something in.

And He did! When we found our promised home, I discovered that God had added a beautiful patio that I wasn't even expecting.

God has always been a "too much" God. And He is faithful to fulfill His promises spoken from the mouths of His people.

While I was declaring His promises regarding our second home, I was still watching children in my

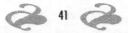

home. When the parents would come to pick up their kids and walk past the posted floor plan, they'd ask, "What's that?" So I always had an opportunity to declare God's promises to others. But the best part about it is that they got to see God bring every single one of those promises to pass.

BE FULLY PERSUADED

Now, it's good to keep God's promises before your face and in your mouth, but there has to come a point where you're not just making a declaration or a confession, but that promise has possession of you.

My eyes were so focused on the promise during that time that I was totally convinced it would happen any day. I mean, I was like Abraham. The Bible says that **he staggered not at the promise of God** but was **fully persuaded that, what he had promised, he was able also to perform** (Rom. 4:20,21).

Sometimes a setback or something would come up and, like David, I would make my soul bless the Lord. I'd say, "Bless the Lord, Cathy. And don't you forget His benefits—*not a one!*" (Ps. 103:2.)

Sometimes you have to do that. Sometimes you have to take hold of your mind, your will and your emotions and say, "You're going to bless the Lord, whether you feel like it or not. You're going to bless Him and declare His promises, no matter what things look like."

You could be in the deepest, darkest cave and it still wouldn't limit God. He is able to bring His Word to pass, whether you're in a cavern, a cottage or the house of your dreams. But you have to make the first step.

I'm a living testimony that if you will follow David's example and keep on declaring God's promises right where you are, God will perform all things for *you.*

CHAPTER 5

§ § §

EXPECT VICTORY AND PRAISE GOD

He shall send from heaven, and save me from the reproach of him that would swallow me up. Selah. God shall send forth his mercy and his truth.

Psalm 57:3

Not only did David boldly declare God's promises over his life, but he expected God to fulfill those

promises. He expected God to deliver him. He expected victory.

David knew God was able and willing to deliver him out of the caves in life. Regardless of the contrary circumstances, David knew God would send forth His mercy and truth. Truth is a powerful force that God sends to those who make Him their refuge and cry out to Him in faith. Once you know the truth of who God is and what He has said in His Word, that truth will set you free. (John 8:32.)

David was ready and fully expecting God to set him free from that cave, and truth was the powerful force that God used to do it.

LAY CLAIM TO DIVINE PROTECTION

David wrote another psalm that was full of truth concerning God's protection: Psalm 91:4. It is one of my favorite verses. It's one of those powerful promises that you can declare no matter how many fiery darts the enemy sends your way.

He shall cover thee with his feathers, and under his wings shalt thou trust: his truth [His Word] **shall be thy shield and buckler.**

Psalm 91:4

When I first read that verse, I remember wondering, *What's a buckler?* So I looked it up and discovered that it's similar to the Hebrew word used for crocodile skin.[1]

A buckler is like armor that covers your entire body. All of a sudden I realized that God's Word was not just a shield in front of me, but it was complete body armor that totally surrounds me, reinforces me and makes me impenetrable to the enemy.

So when those fiery darts come, they just melt off and dissolve because that buckler surrounds me. (Eph. 6:16.) His Word, His truth, is a shield to me. But, praise God, it's also a buckler.

Have you ever seen a picture of one of those shiny suits of armor standing in the corner of some

castle? It almost looks like somebody is in there ready to fight, doesn't it? And even though nobody is inside, it's literally able to stand up on its own because it's so solid and sturdy.

Well, imagine wearing that kind of protection in the time of battle. It would be pretty hard to be knocked down with one of those things on, wouldn't it?

The Word of God is a suit of armor more solid and sturdy than any of those you've ever seen with your physical eyes. Even if you feel like fainting, as though you are so weak you can't go another step, that armor of God's truth will hold you up and strengthen you.

SUPERNATURAL REINFORCEMENTS

When you put faith behind God's Word, the truth of God reinforces and strengthens you. The Word will reinforce everything in your life. It's a powerful tool. It's the force of truth in operation. And when you expect it to work, it will.

In fact, the Bible often talks about God's strengthening His people when we expect Him to fulfill His promises. Psalm 31:24 refers to God's strengthening all those who hope in him.

Be of good courage, and he shall strengthen your heart, all ye that hope in the Lord.

Psalm 31:24

Now, to the natural mind, it seems God has that verse backwards. You almost want to say, "Lord, strengthen my heart so that I *can* be of good courage." But God's truth says it's the other way around: Be of good courage first, and *then* He will strengthen you.

That's a declaration from the throne of God. God is in effect prophesying to you, saying, "Be of good courage!" He's not telling you to do it in yourself. He's declaring a thing, just as when He said, "Light, be." (Gen. 1:3.)

When God uses that word *be,* it's backed with a supernatural creative force. So if He tells you in His Word to *be of good courage* because He will strengthen your heart, and you begin to declare that promise, He sends reinforcements of truth to surround you and cause you to be invincible before the enemy. His truth will do that.

So the fourth thing you need to do when you're in a cave is start feeding on the truth of God, because it will reinforce your hope in Him and enable you, like David, to be of good courage and expect your victory.

PRAISE YOUR GOD

Did you know that you can praise God for the victory even while you're expecting Him to bring you through? That's what David did, and that's the final key to victory found in Psalm 57. Listen to what David said even while he was still in his cave:

My heart is fixed, O God, my heart is fixed: I will sing and give praise.

 50

I will praise thee, O Lord, among the people: I will sing unto thee among the nations.

Be thou exalted, O God, above the heavens: let thy glory be above all the earth.

Psalm 57:7,9,11

Throughout this psalm David talks about singing and giving praise to God.

The men with David heard him sing every morning. They had to listen to his voice, whether they liked it or not. They listened to him sing praises to God and they listened to him sing about singing praises among the nations, though at that point his circumstances weren't much to sing about.

But David said, **O God, my heart is fixed: I will sing and give praise** (v. 7). David's heart was so fixed on God and His promise that he couldn't help but praise Him. And because he learned the power of

praise, he was able to reveal to his generation the God who "performed all things." (v. 2.)

THE WAY OUT OF YOUR CAVE

Praise unlocks the keys of death. Praise unlocks all of heaven to you. God has things for you that you've never even known, and He wants to reveal secrets to you that will pull you out of the cave that you're in and set you free.

I don't know what your situation is, but I do know that God is good, and He'll pick you up when you're down. Only God can turn a shepherd boy into a king, a failure into a success, a loser into a winner. Only He can show you the way out of your cave.

So remember the lessons that David and his mighty men learned. Make God your refuge. Cry out to Him when you're in trouble. Declare His promises every day. Expect to see the victory. And never forget to give God praise. *That's* the way out of the cave and into victory.

If David and the 400 men who followed him into his cave learned to apply these five keys to victory, so can you. And when you do, you won't just be headed for victory; you'll be headed for glory. And God will be glorified because of it.

CHAPTER 6

$\clubsuit$ $\clubsuit$ $\clubsuit$

JONATHAN: YOU CAN'T KEEP A GOOD MAN DOWN

Jonathan, the son of King Saul, is our second caveman. By anybody's standards, Jonathan was a good man. Yet he found himself in a situation where he and his army had to flee and hide in a cave. Despite his cave days, his life proves that old proverbial saying, "You can't keep a good man down."

During the second year of Jonathan's father's reign as king, Saul chose an army of 3000 men. Two thousand were with him in Michmash and 1000 were with Jonathan in Gibeah. (1 Sam. 13:1,2.) According to verse 5, their rivals, the Philistines, also gathered together an army.

The Philistines gathered themselves together to fight with Israel, thirty thousand chariots, and six thousand horsemen, and people as the sand which is on the seashore in multitude: and they came up, and pitched in Michmash, eastward from Bethaven.

Remember, Israel had only 3000 men, while the Philistines were amply supplied with 30,000 chariots and 6000 horsemen, not to mention the people they couldn't count.

With those kinds of odds, what would you do? I'll tell you what *they* did. They ran and hid in a cave!

When the men of Israel saw that they were in a strait, (for the people were distressed,) then the people did hide themselves in caves, and in thickets, and in rocks, and in high places, and in pits.

1 Samuel 13:6

They hid from the enemy because they were terrified for their lives.

LET'S GO!

But the Word says there came a day when Jonathan said to his armor bearer, "Come on; let's go!"

Now it came to pass upon a day, that Jonathan the son of Saul said unto the young man that bare his armour, Come, and let us go over to the Philistines' garrison, that is on the other side. But he told not his father.

1 Samuel 14:1

57

Jonathan had one of those moments. "It came to pass upon a day" that Jonathan said, "Enough is enough!"

There has to be a day or a moment in your life when you take a stand and declare, "Come on; let's go! Let's get out of here. We're not going to stay in this cave anymore."

You have to make a determination that no matter what you've been through or what you're going through now, it's not going to keep you down. There has to be a moment in time when you declare victory; when you decide you've had enough; when you're sick and tired of being sick and tired; when you get up, brush the dust off your feet and go on with Jesus.

GOD IS NOT RESTRAINED

In verse 6, Jonathan said,

Come, and let us go over unto the garrison of these uncircumcised: it may be that the Lord will work for us: for there is no

restraint to the Lord to save by many or by few.

Can you see the heart of Jonathan that day? He said, "There is no restraint to the Lord."

Those words still ring true today. No matter how tiny you are in your own strength, *there is no restraint to God.* He is unlimited. You can't hold Him back. By many or by few, no matter how big the opposition, God is not restrained to save. So nothing is impossible for those who believe.

Well, Jonathan believed and so did his armor bearer—and that's all it took.

YOU'RE NOT IN IT ALONE

God always sends someone to your side to believe and agree with you. Jesus said, **If two of you shall agree on earth as touching any thing that they shall ask, it shall be done for them of my Father which is in heaven. For where two or three are gathered together in my name, there am I in the**

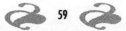

midst of them (Matt. 18:19,20). God always calls someone to be with you so that you can agree in prayer and do all that is within your heart and walk out of your cave victoriously.

In Jonathan's case, that someone was his armor bearer. He told Jonathan, **Do all that is in thine heart: turn thee; behold, I am with thee according to thy heart** (1 Sam. 14:7).

It was a good day to agree with Jonathan, because Jonathan had a God-inspired thought that day. Jonathan had it in his heart that God was going to fight for him. Only God could give someone a thought that says, *Go out, you and your armor bearer, and stand up there against 30,000 chariots, 6,000 horsemen and a mass of people as great as the sand of the sea.* Only God would say that, because only God knew Jonathan wouldn't be standing alone, but He would be standing with God himself as his armor and strength! The moment

Jonathan took that step and stood up for God, God stood with Jonathan.

The apostle Paul also learned that when he stood for God, God would stand with him. And with God on his side, Paul was stronger than any opponent. After he went to prison, he told Timothy, **No man stood with me, but...the Lord stood with me, and strengthened me** (2 Tim. 4:16,17).

And the Lord will stand with you and strengthen you, too, when you step out for Him and declare His Word—because God is a faithful God.

God Can Shake Up and Melt Down

I can picture how this must have happened. Here come Jonathan and his armor bearer climbing up that hill. Then they stand up on the cliff and get right up in the face of those Philistines. First Samuel tells us what happens:

Both of them discovered themselves unto the garrison of the Philistines: and the Philistines said, Behold, the Hebrews come forth out of the holes where they had hid themselves.

And there was trembling in the host, in the field, and among all the people: the garrison, and the spoilers, they also trembled, and the earth quaked: so it was a very great trembling.

And the watchmen of Saul in Gibeah of Benjamin looked; and, behold, the multitude melted away, and they went on beating down one another.

1 Samuel 14:11,15,16

I believe when Jonathan and his armor bearer stood up on that hill, they weren't standing in their own strength. I believe they were surrounded by that armor, that buckler system of God, and the Philistines didn't see little Jonathan that day—they saw an army of God!

The Philistines were shocked. They said to themselves, *The Israelites have come out of their caves and their holes!* And those Philistines started to tremble. God just shook them up and melted them down.

Saul and his army over in Gibeah looked, and they saw that the people had melted away.

Now, when I think of something melting away, I think about pictures I've seen of an atomic bomb explosion. A force goes up and then the wind flows against the surface of the earth and melts away everything in its path.

That's how I see the power of the anointing of God. His anointing in Jonathan's life that day was so strong that it melted away the army assembled against the children of Israel.

SEND THE DEVIL A SHOCK WAVE

Do you know that when *you* obey God's commands and walk in boldness, the enemy trembles? And when you stand up in the strength of God and declare His promises, saying, "God is not restrained to save by many or by few," God just melts away all those problems in your life.

So take courage. Be strong and very courageous and step out of that cave. I'm telling you, God is going to step out with you. He's going to reinforce and strengthen you with truth so that you walk out and your enemies just fall flat before you. And when that happens, all the glory will go to God!

The enemy doesn't want you to know this. This is the kind of thing that sends him trembling and running off into a cave himself.

Don't you know faith in God sends shock waves of panic through the enemy's camp? Jesse and I just love shocking the devil. No matter how we feel or

how things look, we just declare God's Word and boldly step out in faith.

One time Jesse served notice on the devil because hurricanes were trying to hit our area. Well, we're in the process of building a seven- million-dollar ministry complex, so Jesse told the devil, "If you try to destroy those buildings, you're going to owe me forty-nine million dollars. I just wanted to let you know."

I tell you, that sent shock waves through the enemy's camp, and he ran away!

You can cause the same thing to happen when you stand with God. You just have to know who you are in Jesus and serve notice on the devil. Tell him if he dares to touch anything in your house, he's going to have to repay you sevenfold. That's right, Proverbs 6:30-31 says a thief must restore sevenfold!

I'm telling you, with the Word as your buckler, you can be so strong that no matter what tries to keep you down, you keep getting back up. And with faith

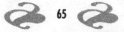

in God, you can do some serious damage to the enemy.

The devil can't stand it. That's why he wants to oppress you and get you discouraged and keep you in a cave. He knows the minute you come out of that cave, his days are numbered. He knows that God is going to be glorified and that he himself is going to be shoved in a cave.

Now, it would seem if the devil knew *that* much, he ought to be able to figure out by now that you can't keep a good man down!

CHAPTER 7

§ § §

ELIJAH: GOD IS NOT THROUGH WITH YOU

Some things can attack you and push you so far into a cave that you can't even see the impact of your life anymore. You don't feel like you're doing much of anything. This was the case for the prophet Elijah, our third caveman.

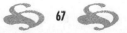 67

It was also the case for a pastor in whose church Jesse used to preach yearly revivals. This pastor had a strong, small church, but he didn't feel like he was making much of an impact in the kingdom of God.

At a point in his life when he was feeling very low, he looked at his congregation and said, "All my desires and dreams to do something great for God have never really been fulfilled. I'm not doing anything. I'm not reaching the thousands that I envisioned earlier in my ministry."

Not too long ago that preacher passed away. Jesse heard about his funeral and that there must have been close to 10,000 people there. The whole town shut down.

Jesse heard story after story of people whose lives were changed because of this pastor. He had impacted so many people's lives, and through his ministry God had produced so much fruit, but he never saw it.

It's sad, but many great men and women of God don't ever recognize how valuable they are to the kingdom of God and how terrifying they really are to the devil.

So often we don't see beyond our present circumstances, so we get discouraged, thinking we're not being as effective as we'd like to be. But if we could just take a look into the spiritual realm, we'd see the impact we're making because we are being obedient to do the very thing that God called us to do.

FROM THE TREE OF DESPAIR TO THE CAVE OF DEPRESSION

When we read about Elijah in 1 Kings 19, we see that he was at a very low point in his life too. He was so depressed that he wanted to die. Jezebel had sent word that she was going to kill him, so he was running for his life.

The Bible says he fled into the wilderness, sat under a juniper tree and said in despair, **It is enough;**

now, O Lord, take away my life; for I am not better than my fathers (1 Kings 19:4).

If Elijah really wanted to die, he could have just stuck around, because Jezebel would have taken care of that! But an angel of the Lord came to Elijah and ministered to him until he was strong enough to go up to Mount Horeb, the place where God spoke to Moses out of the burning bush, and the only place the Bible calls holy ground. (Ex. 3:4,5.) It was also the place where God gave His covenant to His people. (Deut. 5:2.)

So in his despair and at the lowest point in his life, Elijah ran to Mount Horeb to get back to that place where God spoke to His people. Then, according to 1 Kings 19:9,

> **He came thither unto a cave, and lodged there; and, behold, the word of the Lord came to him, and he said unto him, What doest thou here, Elijah?**

So Elijah hid out in a cave, depressed and convinced that the voice of the Lord wasn't going forth in the earth. Then God spoke to him and asked him, "What are you doing here?"

Now, Elijah could have said, "I'm here because this is holy ground, Lord. This is where You spoke to us and gave us Your covenant. I want to be with You and hear Your voice." But instead, he said despondently, **The children of Israel have forsaken thy covenant, thrown down thine altars, and slain thy prophets with the sword; and I, even I only, am left; and they seek my life, to take it away** (v. 10).

In other words, he said, "Here I am, Lord, the only one serving You. There's nobody else left but me, and they're trying to kill me."

Later God told him, "Look, Elijah, I have 7000 who haven't bowed their knees to Baal." (v. 18.)

 71

Remember that when you start thinking you're the last prophet in the land, God always has a remnant of people who are trusting in Him.

But even though Elijah was at this low point of despair, God still had a plan for his life. Elijah just couldn't see it.

When you yield to depression, it blinds you to the truth and gives you a distorted view of life. That's the kind of view Elijah had that day. He was blinded by depression.

GOD WANTS TO GIVE YOU WORDS

But God wanted to show him a way out, so He gave him words of hope.

He said, Go forth, and stand upon the mount before the Lord. And, behold, the Lord passed by, and a great and strong wind rent the mountains, and brake in pieces the rocks before the Lord; but the Lord was not in the wind: and after the

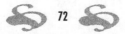

wind an earthquake; but the Lord was not in the earthquake: and after the earthquake a fire; but the Lord was not in the fire: and after the fire a still small voice.

And it was so, when Elijah heard it, that he wrapped his face in his mantle, and went out, and stood in the entering in of the cave. And, behold, there came a voice unto him, and said, What doest thou here, Elijah?

1 Kings 19:11-13

God restored Elijah and strengthened him that day. And then He commissioned him and gave him something to do. (v. 15.)

No matter how far you run or where you hide, God always knows how to get to your heart. He always knows how to speak words that will lift you up.

It was when Elijah heard the Lord speaking in the still, small voice that he started taking steps to come out of that cave. But he wanted to stay and abide in

the presence of God so much that he just stood there awhile, his face wrapped in his mantle, listening to God's instructions and words of hope.

Right in the midst of the cave of your depression, God wants to give you words of hope. He wants you to know that He is not through with you. You may have been so blinded by the distractions of the enemy that you don't even know which step to take next or where to go. But He wants to restore your strength and reveal answers to you that will lead you out of that dark place.

God wants to give words to you—*still, small voice* words that will restore your strength and equip you. Then He'll send you out victorious, because He has a plan for your life and He still has something for you to do.

You Still Have Work To Do

Have you stepped out ahead of God? Have you done something that you shouldn't have done? Do

you feel like you just want to give up now and not go forward anymore?

Don't do it! Don't run into a cave and hide out forever. God wasn't through with Elijah and He's not through with you.

But even if you have given up on yourself, God has not given up on you. Even though you may have failed at some point, God still has work for you to do.

Even though Elijah ran and hid in a cave, God still had great things for him to do. He had a plan for Elijah's life.

And Elijah went on to do amazing things. He came out of that cave in Mount Horeb and went and laid his mantle on Elisha, anointing him for ministry. (v. 19.) He went back in Ahab's face and rebuked him; then he prophesied to him about the death of Ahab's wife, Jezebel, and son, Ahaziah. (1 Kings 21:17-26; 2 Kings 1:4.) He called down fire from heaven on 100 of Ahaziah's soldiers and 2 of his captains. (vv. 9-12.)

God used Elijah up until the very end. Right before he was taken up to heaven in a whirlwind, he divided the river Jordan with his mantle. (2 Kings 2:8.) In fact, the anointing on Elijah was so strong that Elisha received a double portion. (vv. 9-15.) And that anointing on Elisha was so powerful that when they buried a man on top of his bones, the man rose from the dead! (2 Kings 13:20,21.)

God's anointing is not only tangible, it's transferable. I'm telling you, the anointing God placed upon Elijah at the mouth of the cave, when he was wrapped up in that mantle, was so powerful it changed people's lives even long after he had gone in that glorious whirlwind. (2 Kings 2:11.)

You may have given up on yourself, but I want you to know that God hasn't given up on you. He still has something for you to do. He wants to reveal secrets that will get you out of that cave and put you on a path that will set you and others around you free.

That's why you can't stay in that cave: God wants to use you. He's not through with you yet!

CHAPTER 8

$\mathfrak{S}\ \mathfrak{S}\ \mathfrak{S}$

NO MORE RUNNING
AND HIDING

I n this book I've given you several examples of men in the Bible, because if you're stuck in a cave, you need to hear how someone else went through the same thing and made it out all right. I wanted to lay a strong foundation from the Word to begin with, because it's the Word that will be your buckler through any trial. But I learned something years ago

in those testimony services at that little church where I was born again: Sometimes someone's personal testimony can bless and inspire you as nothing else can.

I want to share with you some more things from my own life now, in faith that you will be inspired to come out of your cave and enter into victory.

I Wanted a Cave To Hide In

Sometimes people look at me and think that I've never been through anything. But let me tell you, I've had moments in my life when I felt like I was in a cave or, at least, I wanted to get in one.

I remember one time when I was with Jesse at a meeting in Capetown, South Africa. They had just finished introducing Jesse and I heard him say, "My wife is here. I'd like her to come up and say a few words for the Lord."

I made it up the stairs to the platform by myself, even though they were pretty steep and short. Then I preached a few minutes and turned to leave.

Now, I could have walked down those steps gracefully and gone back to my seat on the front row, but I didn't exactly do that. I started walking and the heel of my shoe caught the edge of the first step. I don't know if something was sticking out of the carpeting or what, but the next thing I knew, I was hurtling down those stairs.

I braced myself for the inevitable, thinking, *I'm about to fall on my face and splatter across the floor in front of 2000 people!* Then, right at the last possible moment, the pastor rose up and caught my hand.

He caught me just in time. I landed on both my knees with a thud and tore my stockings. But thank God I didn't fall on my face.

There I was, trying to be graceful, and I wound up falling into the arms of the pastor. I was so embar-

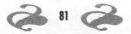

rassed. I wished the floor could have opened up and swallowed me right then. I thought, *Where's a good dark cave when you need one?*

Of course, Jesse made jokes about it for the rest of the night. He didn't let me get away with that. He pumped that thing for all it was worth: "Yes, she looks younger than I am, but at least I'm not falling down...."

You learn to joke about things like that and not let them get to you. But I didn't think it was very funny at the time. And even though I was saved from being seriously hurt, it was one of those moments in life that I would have liked to have passed on by.

So, yes, I've had some really embarrassing moments in my life (you know, the kind you try your best to forget), but I'm sure everybody has.

Distressing situations come from the enemy, and you can't just run and hide from them. God wants you to come out victorious even in those times. He wants to take your hand and pull you up and out of your place of pain or discouragement.

The devil may have a plan for your defeat, but God always has a plan for your victory. So you just have to go on. Even when *you* mess up, you have to pick yourself up, dust your feet off, stand up and go on. You can't let it get you down.

RUNNING FROM THE ENEMY

Now it's one thing to want to run from embarrassment, but it's another thing to have to run for your life. David, Jonathan and Elijah ran and hid from the enemy because they were terrified for their lives.

I remember a time in my life when I ran and hid from what I considered to be the enemy. My first memories of hiding away are from when I was about fourteen years old, living in a violent home. During those times I knew what it was like to live in a cave.

I didn't know God at the time, so I didn't have the Word of God to draw upon. But God still protected my life.

My mom and dad used to fight all the time. There were six of us kids, and we grew up always hearing our parents yell. Their fighting could get really violent sometimes. One time my dad threw my mom out of a moving car and broke her arm. I have memories of the six of us huddling together, hiding away from them, not wanting to hear all the screaming and fighting

My mom married a second time, and my stepfather was a drunk. (He lived with a can of beer in his hand.) We never understood why he became so violent at times. Every now and then he would act crazy—I mean *really* crazy. One time we came home from school and found all our clothes in the front yard, torn up with a knife. We often wondered what would have happened to us if we'd been home.

We didn't find out until after he died that he had been on heroin from time to time. So God protected my family and me from him many, *many* times.

One time I was sitting on the side of the couch watching TV with my stepfather. No one else was home, and he began to put his arm around me. Then he started trying to touch me in places he shouldn't be touching and saying things he shouldn't be saying to a fourteen-year-old girl.

I was so scared, I ran out of the house and hid in the bushes around the corner. I stayed there for hours until it was dark and my family came home. I didn't know what else to do. I was just hiding away from the enemy.

So often things hit our lives and we hide spiritually because we don't know what to do. We're so weak in our own spiritual strength because maybe we don't know the Lord. That's how I was.

None of us had ever seen that side of our stepfather, so my mom never thought to be careful or

wonder about our being alone with him. But I look back now and I know that, though my mom didn't know to protect me, *God* protected me. I'm thankful for that.

I didn't mention what happened that day until years later. I remember finally telling my mom about it, and she and I never spoke about it again.

GOD WANTS TO CLEAN OUT THE CAVES

I never shared it publicly because it's a part of my past that's under the blood. But the Lord has recently allowed me to start talking about it some to help people who are hiding in deep caves and struggling with those kinds of issues in their lives.

So often traumatic things happen to us and we shove them in a deep, dark part of our lives—way back in the hidden cave of our hearts. We push them away as though they could never affect us again. But God wants to clean even those areas out.

You may not be in a physical cave, but there may be things that have happened in your life that have caused you to retreat. There may be things that have kept you from being yourself or what God wants you to be. But I'm telling you, God can strengthen you and bring you up into a new place in Him.

GOD WANTS TO REVEAL HIS SECRETS TO YOU

Let me tell you what God wants to do. He wants to restore you. He wants to bring you into a new place and show you how strong you are in Him. He wants to reveal secrets that will bring you out of your cave and send you on in victory.

Daniel 2:28 says that there is a God in heaven who reveals secrets. I believe God wants to bring each and every one of us close to His Spirit, day by day, so that He can reveal secrets that will transform our lives.

We may not know all the answers in the natural. You can't just pick up a manual that gives you a five-

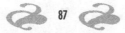

step plan on how to get out of the problems in your life. But God's Word can reveal the secrets to your stepping out of those problems and into His glory.

God's Spirit within us can illuminate golden nuggets of truth and reveal treasures hidden in the Word that will bring us out and cause us to be victorious every day of our lives. And I found out, through my personal experiences and in studying His Word, that that is what He really wants—to bring us out of our caves and into victory.

You have to remember that it's the thief that comes to steal, kill and destroy; but when Jesus comes on the scene, He brings abundant life. (John 10:10.) Jesus is the only one who can turn a life that's bound by fear and oppression into a life that's free and strong in Him.

So you don't have to retreat or stay hidden in a cave. You can come out of discouragement or despair and stand as a strong soldier in the Lord, fully clothed with His armor and strength.

No matter what has happened to you in the past or what you may be currently going through, God has a way to bring you to victory. He has a plan to set you on high and lift you up and show the devil once and for all that every time he tries to attack you, God will deliver you.

Do What David, Jonathan and Elijah Did— Get Ready To Come Out!

If you're looking for a way out of your cave, there is something you can do to pull yourself out. Do what David did. Make God your refuge. Cry out to Him and declare His promises. Then expect to receive the victory as you give praise to God.

Do what Jonathan did. Make a determination once and for all that God is not restrained and nothing is impossible for you. Then take that first step out in faith, knowing that even if no one else stands

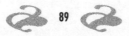

with you, God will stand with you and strengthen you.

Do what Elijah did. Get to a place where you can hear God's words to you and spend time wrapped up in His presence. Then let God's anointing restore and strengthen you so that you go out in His power to do what He wants you to do.

That's how you behave in a cave. And when you learn how to behave in a cave, you won't be there long. Your days in there are numbered. You can pack your bags and say, "I'm coming out!"

In fact, you can just leave all that baggage behind because God's going to give you new stuff. When you walk out of that cave, you're going to be equipped with everything you need to walk forward in victory so that God can be glorified in your life.

ENDNOTES

§ § §

Chapter 3

[1] Charles Finney, *The Autobiography of Charles G. Finney,* Ed. Helen Wessel (Minneapolis: Bethany House, 1977), 37-40, 80-83.

[2] Paul Lee Tan, *Encyclopedia of 7706 Illustrations: Signs of the Times,* (Rockville, Maryland: Assurance Publishers, 1979), 1511.

[3] Ibid.

[4] Ibid., 1675.

Chapter 5

[1] *Biblesoft's New Exhaustive Strong's Numbers and Concordance with Expanded Greek-Hebrew Dictionary* (Biblesoft and International Bible Translators, 1994), entries 4043, 5507.

About the Author

Cathy Duplantis is a fiery, anointed minister of the Gospel who is dedicated to living by faith and teaching others to do the same. The wife of Evangelist Jesse Duplantis, Cathy has worked continually with her husband in the ministry since it began in 1978, serving as Administrator, Editor-in-Chief of *Voice of the Covenant* magazine and television co-host. Cathy continues to preach the Gospel along with Jesse in their *Celebrate Jesus* revival meetings held throughout the USA and has also become a favorite guest speaker for women's conferences and church meetings.

Through these many years, Cathy has encouraged thousands of believers to realize their potential in Christ Jesus, overcome life's circumstances and experience success spiritually, emotionally and physically. Her practical, step-by-step method of teaching has helped many receive exactly what they need from God.

Through revival meetings, television, tapes and printed page, Cathy continues to spread the Gospel around the world and show believers everywhere how they can be transformed into powerful and joyful people of faith by applying the teachings of God's Word.

To contact Cathy Duplantis,

write to:

Cathy Duplantis

c/o Jesse Duplantis Ministries

P.O. Box 20149

New Orleans, Louisiana 70141

(504) 764-2000

www.jdm.org

Please include your prayer requests
and comments when you write.

Additional copies of this book

arc available from your local bookstore.

HARRISON HOUSE

Tulsa, Oklahoma 74153

THE HARRISON HOUSE VISION

Proclaiming the truth and the power

Of the Gospel of Jesus Christ

With excellence;

Challenging Christians to

Live victoriously,

Grow spiritually,

Know God intimately.